Edward Teller and the Development of the Hydrogen Bomb

John Bankston

Mitchell Lane
PUBLISHERS

PO Box 619
Bear, Delaware 19701

Unlocking the Secrets of Science

Profiling 20th Century Achievers in Science, Medicine, and Technology

Edward Teller and the Development of the Hydrogen Bomb

Copyright © 2002 by Mitchell Lane Publishers, Inc. All rights reserved. No part of this book may be reproduced without written permission from the publisher. Printed and bound in the United States of America.

First Printing

Library of Congress Cataloging-in-Publication Data
Bankston, John, 1974-
   Edward Teller and the development of the hydrogen bomb / John Bankston.
        p.cm. — (Unlocking the secrets of science)
Includes bibliographical references and index.
Summary: A biography of the Hungarian-born Jewish physicist whose work in developing the atomic and hydrogen bombs, as well as the weapons system known as Strategic Defense Initiative, still generates controversy.
   ISBN 1-58415-108-0
1. Teller, Edward, 1908—Juvenile literature. 2. Physicists—United States—Biography—Juvenile literature. 3. Atomic bomb—United States—History—Juvenile literature. 4. Hydrogen bomb—History—Juvenile literature. [1. Teller, Edward, 1908- 2. Physicists. 3. Manhattan Project (U.S.) 4. Atomic bomb. 5. Hydrogen bomb. 6. Strategic Defense Initiative. 7. Jews—Biography.] I. Title. II. Series.
   QC16.T37 B36 2001
   539.7'092—dc21
                                                                      2001038709

ABOUT THE AUTHOR: Born in Boston, Massachusetts, John Bankston began publishing articles in newspapers and magazines while still a teenager. Since then, he has written over two hundred articles, and contributed chapters to books such as *Crimes of Passion* and *Death Row 2000*, which have been sold in bookstores around the world. He has recently written a number of biographies for Mitchell Lane including books on Mandy Moore, Jessica Simpson and Jonas Salk. He currently lives in Los Angeles, California, pursuing a career in the entertainment industry. He has worked as a writer for the movies Dot-Com and the upcoming *Planetary Suicide*, which begins filming in 2002. As an actor John has appeared in episodes of *Sabrina the Teenage Witch*, *Charmed* and *Get Real* along with appearances in the films *Boys and Girls*, and *America So Beautiful*. He has a supporting part in *Planetary Suicide* and has recently completed his first young adult novel, *18 To Look Younger*.

PHOTO CREDITS: cover: Science Photo Library; p. 6. Hulton/Archive; p. 10 Archive Photos; p. 18 Hulton/Getty; p. 23 AP Photo; p.24 Hulton/Getty; p. 30 Hulton/Getty; p. 40 Globe Photos; p. 48 AP Photo.

PUBLISHER'S NOTE: In selecting those persons to be profiled in this series, we first attempted to identify the most notable accomplishments of the 20th century in science, medicine, and technology. When we were done, we noted a serious deficiency in the inclusion of women. For the greater part of the 20th century science, medicine, and technology were male-dominated fields. In many cases, the contributions of women went unrecognized. Women have tried for years to be included in these areas, and in many cases, women worked side by side with men who took credit for their ideas and discoveries. Even as we move forward into the 21st century, we find women still sadly underrepresented. It is not an oversight, therefore, that we profiled mostly male achievers. Information simply does not exist to include a fair selection of women.

Contents

Some of the American scientists who were instrumental in developing the atomic bomb gathered to celebrate the opening of the Institute of Nuclear Studies and Institute of Metals at the University of Chicago on June 9, 1945. Standing l to r: Edward Teller, Thorfin Hogness, Walter Zinn, and Clarence Zener. Seated l to r: W. H. Zachariasen, Harlod Urey, and Cyril Smith.

Chapter 1
Controversy

● ●

Scientists who make discoveries are often controversial. That is because they are often going against an established set of beliefs and trying to prove them wrong. Since many people disagree with them, controversy is inevitable.

In 1530, a Polish clergyman named Nicolaus Copernicus published his great work *De Revolutionibus*, which advanced the belief that the earth rotated on its axis daily and completed one complete revolution of the sun annually. His ideas were controversial to the people of the 16th century, and the church considered them heresy. Seventy years later Giordano Bruno, who took Copernicus' ideas even further, was burned at the stake. And Galileo Galilei, who used the telescope he invented to try to prove that Copernicus was right, was threatened with torture and death if he didn't recant—admit that he was wrong.

Today Copernicus and his point of view are no longer controversial because it has long been established that the earth revolves around the sun.

In 1859, Charles Darwin published his book *The Origin of Species*, which advanced what is now known as the theory of evolution. He was widely ridiculed at the time, but today most scientists believe—with some modifications—that he was correct.

In the twentieth century, Jonas Salk was controversial before he proved the effectiveness of his polio vaccine; afterwards the public hailed him as a hero. Whenever scientists discover a cure for a dreaded disease or a way to travel to the stars or explore the depths of the ocean, they are often greeted with nearly universal admiration even though their ideas may not have been accepted at first.

The pioneers of the atomic age are different. The people who worked on the Manhattan Project, which unleashed the awesome power of the atom, created a weapon capable of unimaginable destruction. Over fifty years later, they are still controversial despite their discoveries.

Among this group, it would be difficult to find someone more controversial than Edward Teller, who is often called "the father of the hydrogen bomb." A Hungarian immigrant, a man who fled Germany during the Nazi regime and successfully proved that the atom bomb could be used without creating a world-destroying chain reaction, he is even more controversial today than he was in the 1950s when the first H-bomb was produced.

Edward Teller is a man who believes that what he did saved lives. He believes the discoveries he made changed the world for the better.

"I am still asked on occasion whether I am not sorry for having invented such a terrible thing as the hydrogen bomb," he wrote in *Science* magazine. "The answer is, I am not."

But his choices and his beliefs have been questioned not just by citizens and government officials, but also by his fellow scientists. Many abandoned him, refusing to go along with his post-World War II ambitions for a weapon even more powerful than the atomic bomb created by the Manhattan Project pioneers.

Beginning in the 1960s, he was a leader in developing what is now known as the Strategic Defense Initiative, a weapons system which remains front page news. The system, sometimes called "Star Wars," is considered by some to be the next logical step for a safer world. Yet just as many people believe Teller's latest dream is dangerous to consider, expensive to develop and impossible to build.

Edward Teller is embraced as a genius who helped make the world a safer place, and hated as the person who developed a weapon 1,000 times more destructive than the first atomic bomb. One winner of the Nobel Prize in physics described him as "one of the most thoughtful statesmen of science," while another said that he was "a danger to all that's important."

And I. I. Rabi, a man who worked closely with him to develop the atomic bomb said, "It would be a better world without Teller."

So it's not too surprising that when he suffered a stroke a few years ago and checked into the hospital, a nurse asked him, "Are you the famous Edward Teller?"

"No," he replied. "I'm the infamous Edward Teller."

But regardless of the opinion that people have of him, his impact on the twentieth century is undeniable.

Often called the "father of the hydrogen bomb," Edward Teller believes the device he helped invent, with its potential to kill millions of people, actually made the world a safer place.

Chapter 2
The Silent Child

• •

The toddler wasn't talking. He loved to walk, to play, to explore, but he never spoke. He was already three, and his parents were worried. His sister Emmi was just twenty months older, but she'd been speaking for years.

Edward Teller had been born to Max and Ilona Teller on January 15, 1908 in Budapest, Hungary. Max was a successful lawyer, Ilona a talented pianist from a prominent banking family.

So even though Edward was a bright and happy child, his parents were worried. According to one account, Edward's grandfather even quietly told Ilona, "I think you have to prepare yourself for the possibility that you have a retarded child." He couldn't have been more wrong.

Because one day when he was almost four, little Edward just started talking. And talking. He skipped "baby talk" and went right to whole sentences, using words that many adults have to look up in a dictionary. He surpassed children twice his age.

Instead of counting sheep to fall asleep, he started doing math problems.

"I was about five years old, maybe not five years old yet," Teller told the American Academy of Achievement in a recent interview. "I was supposed to go to sleep and didn't and I invented a game. I was trying to find out how many seconds in an hour or in a day or in a year. And that, of course, obviously, I did in my head. Quite naturally I got different answers in my head every time I did it. And that made the game more interesting."

Math problems and conversation weren't the only ways Edward filled his days. His mother Ilona began to teach her son to play the piano. He learned quickly and for a time she was certain her child would be another Wolfgang Amadeus Mozart, the 18th century Austrian composer who began performing piano concertos at an age when most children begin grade school.

But it was not to be.

"Practicing piano was much too hard," Teller told the American Academy of Achievement. "Multiplying numbers was not."

So instead of at concerts, young Teller gained his attention at school. Unfortunately it wasn't all good.

At five he began attending the nearby Mellinger School. Unlike many children his age, he wasn't intimidated by his teachers. Edward would argue with *anyone* he believed was wrong. Many of his classmates thought he was a know-it-all. Some of the older ones would regularly beat him up on the way home from school.

Instead of going to his parents or to a teacher, Teller devised his own solution to the problem.

One night he attached a long leather strap to his book bag. The next day his tormentors blocked his path. Edward began swinging his bag. Heavy with books, the leather satchel easily knocked down boys twice his size. After that, the bigger kids left him alone. For young Teller, the experience provided a valuable lesson: A powerful weapon can make the size and number of an enemy unimportant.

At home, Edward was equally unafraid of his parents. At dinner time, he'd drift into his own little world, barely noticing them when they asked him a question. If they tried to start a conversation with him, he'd often say, "Please don't talk to me, I have a problem."

"It was more of a plea than rudeness," his sister Emmi would recall years later in a Teller biography written by Stanley Blumberg and Louis Panostold. "He would say it very politely and he would apologize. We knew he was thinking about something he considered very important at the time and we understood."

Outside the Teller home, a crisis was developing. On June 28, 1914, the Archduke Franz Ferdinand, heir to the throne of Austria-Hungary, was assassinated in Sarajevo, Serbia. Austria-Hungary suspected that the government of Serbia had helped the assassin and, supported by Germany, sent an ultimatum to Serbia.

The response was hostile.

So Austria-Hungary declared war. But Serbia was allied with Russia, and Russian troops mobilized along the Austrian border. The situation quickly escalated into war. Because most European countries had signed treaties with one side or the other, they were dragged into the conflict and it became known as the Great War, or World War I. Across the ocean, the United States and Canada would eventually be involved as well.

In Budapest, food became scarce. Edward's father continued to earn a living, but times were difficult. The streets outside their home were dangerous, and Edward's school shut down. Despite the hardships, he studied at home, managing to complete the four-year course with honors in the spring of 1918.

By then, the war was ending. In Russia, a communist revolution had already unseated the Czar, who had been like a king. The communists believed in a one-party system where industry is owned by the state and freedoms of the press and speech are limited. And they believed that other countries should have the same system of government.

So when the Austro-Hungarian monarchy fell at the end of the war and Hungary became a separate country, communists led by Bela Kun took over its government for a brief period in 1919. The changes they made, which included killing people who disagreed with them, quickly aroused opposition and four months later they were overthrown by forces led by Admiral Nicholas Horthy.

For Edward's family, the new system created challenges as difficult as those faced during the war. Although not very religious, the Tellers were Jewish and anti-Semitism—hatred of the Jews—was a part of the Horthy government's philosophy.

"My father was a lawyer; his office was occupied and shut down and occupied by the Reds [communists]. But what followed was an anti-Semitic Fascist regime, and I was at least as opposed to the Fascists as I was to the Communists," he said in an interview in *Scientific American* magazine.

Despite these upheavals, Edward still enjoyed his home life. He considered math problems, and escaped into the writings of 19th century French novelist Jules Verne. Verne's futuristic descriptions of spaceships and rocket rides to the moon inspired many future scientists like Teller.

At school, Teller's life was not as calm. In the autumn of 1918, he had begun attending the Minta Gymnasium, a respected school which emphasized Latin and other classical subjects. As he had in elementary school, Teller continued to upset teachers and fellow students by always questioning and arguing.

In one instance, Teller's teacher began discussing advanced algebra using a problem the class hadn't seen yet. As Teller would recall years later to his biographers, "I put up my hand. [The teacher] asked and I answered. And then he asked me, 'What are you, a repeater?'"

The teacher was convinced Teller had taken the course before. How else could he have known the answer to such a complicated problem? After Teller told the teacher he'd never studied algebra, the teacher refused to ever call on him again.

Edward wasn't discouraged. He had a strong belief in his own abilities—so strong he refused to let the opinions of others deter him from following his own dreams. Even his father couldn't change his mind.

One night, Max Teller watched as Edward helped his older sister with her homework. Instead of being proud of his son's abilities, Max was worried. He was afraid his son would grow up to be a teacher. To Edward's father, the profession was a miserable choice. Teaching meant long hours, low pay and little prestige.

In order to discourage Edward, Max invited Leopold Klug, a family friend who taught mathematics at the University of Budapest, to spend some time with his son.

Instead of convincing the teen to pursue another dream, Leopold's attention encouraged Edward. According to Teller's biography, Leopold Klug told Edward's father that "Your son is exceptional" after just six sessions with the teenager.

"Klug was the first grown up whom I met who loved what he was doing," Teller recalled in his interview with the American Academy of Achievement. "He even enjoyed explaining things to me. That, I think, is when I made up my mind very firmly that I wanted to do something that I really did want to do. Not for anyone else's sake, not for what it might lead to, but because of my inherent interest in the subject."

At school, Edward Teller worked hard at getting top grades and finally even earning the respect of his peers. Despite his accomplishments, his father refused to believe in Edward's dreams. Max Teller loved his son, and he wanted Edward to be happy. It was just that he felt there was no way Edward would have a stable, successful life pursuing a career in mathematics. Besides his obvious concerns about how low-paying teaching was, Max was also worried Edward might never get a job in Hungary at all. The government had imposed a quota system. Universities were only allowed to accept a few Jewish people as teachers.

The Teller home became a battlefield. Father and son were both equally stubborn and equally convinced they were right.

Teller's mother, Ilona, wasn't concerned about the profession her son chose. She believed he'd be successful at whatever he tried. She was more worried about him leaving. Because she wasn't ready for Edward to go, she wanted him to enroll at the nearby University of Budapest and live at home.

In the end, Edward did what both of his parents wanted him to do. He took the exams for enrollment at the University of Budapest and agreed to stay at his parents' house.

When he tested the highest in his class in the math and physics exams, he was certain his father would see his side of things. He was wrong. Max Teller was just as certain that his son would need a more practical education than mathematics. He made his son enroll in the university as an engineering major. To Max, *that* was a career with a real future.

In the fall of 1925, Edward Teller began his studies at the University of Budapest, wondering if all his dreams were behind him.

More than a scientist, Albert Einstein was both a hero and a celebrity. His famous equation $E=mc^2$ would have perhaps more influence on science than any other 20th century theory.

Chapter 3
Standing Up to Dad

• •

Forced to enroll at a school he didn't want to attend and major in a subject he didn't like, Edward Teller felt like the unhappiest young man alive. Studies at the University of Budapest were boring and his only joy came from outside of school.

Edward Teller was slowly falling in love.

A few months before he graduated from the Minta, he'd begun seeing the sister of Edward Harkanyi, his best friend. Augusta Maria was a pretty sixteen-year-old with a sharp mind and a quick wit. Nicknamed Mici, the young girl started out as Edward's friend, but over the next year the friendship developed into something more.

At that point in his life, Edward needed all the happiness he could find. For as 1925 faded and the fall semester ended, Edward Teller had had enough.

During the break between semesters, he confronted his father, telling him that he needed to study math, that it was his love and he was certain it would eventually lead somewhere.

But Max Teller wasn't just going to give up and let his only son throw his life away on a dream.

"I had to study something real," Edward Teller remembered his father saying. In his interview with the American Academy of Achievement, Teller recalls, "We settled on a compromise. It was to study chemical engineering. This was not completely unreasonable. At least two older Hungarians who became very famous had done the same thing." These men were John Von Neumann, who paved the way for high speed computers, and Eugene Wigner, who helped develop nuclear reactors.

So New Year's Day 1926 dawned with Edward Teller preparing to leave his parents' house and board a train for Karlsruhe in southwest Germany. He was looking forward to his first taste of independence.

In many ways, it was the perfect moment to be in Germany. Although the nation had been severely damaged economically by World War I and the penalties extracted under the Treaty of Versailles which ended the war, the cultural and scientific communities were stronger than ever.

Among the best-known figures in the scientific community was a man Teller had begun reading about before he was even a teenager: Albert Einstein. In 1905, Einstein had developed his theory of relativity. Einstein's theory, expressed as the famous equation $E=mc^2$, holds that energy and matter are convertible into each other. It would have more impact on the lives of twentieth century scientists than almost any other concept.

Herman Mark was in his twenties when he became one of Edward Teller's professors at Karlsruhe Institute of Technology. After describing his former pupil as "stubby and fat" in an interview with Teller's biographers, Mark went on to say, "But if he wasn't handsome, he was always kind. Teller was popular too. The other students respected him. Very frequently during a lecture he would say, 'Well, I think that was very interesting but if you don't mind, I presume what you really wanted to tell us was this.' And he'd explain his idea in a Hungarian accent and he was always right."

Mark, unlike Teller's earlier teachers, wasn't threatened by his student's superior intelligence. A good thing, because being right meant everything to the young man.

Despite his gifts, Teller was challenged by his new school. As a result of the compromise with his father, he was studying chemical engineering *and* mathematics. But two major courses of study meant that he had to work harder than ever before.

"I studied virtually all the time," he told his biographers. "I broke a lot of test tubes, cut my fingers and nearly put my eye out on one occasion."

Then, despite his love for mathematics, Teller found a new passion: physics.

Physics, the study of matter and energy and the way the two interact, was a fairly new discipline. It was led by men like Einstein and Max Planck, whose theories on radiation and energy were published in 1900. As Teller read more and more about physics, he knew this was something he wanted to devote his life to. Unfortunately his father, who was paying Teller's tuition bills and living expenses, had the final say.

When Edward told his father about his new-found passion, Max Teller wasn't pleased. If mathematics was a poor career choice, physics was even worse. His son's flights of fancy were getting ridiculous, and he refused to just let Edward abandon one major for another.

In the end, Teller once again talked his father into a compromise. As a lawyer, Max Teller was used to winning arguments in courtrooms, but he was no match for his son.

In 1928, Teller transferred to yet another school. He was convinced the University of Munich would give him what he wanted. Although his academic life seemed to be in turmoil, his social life was far more stable. During numerous trips back home, Teller had grown closer to Mici. By 1928 the two were exclusive.

When not going home to visit his girlfriend and his parents, Teller filled his free time with hikes around Munich. When he was alone, Edward enjoyed the solitude these long walks provided. They gave him a chance to think about his plans, his studies, and his life. When he went with friends, the explorations were more rowdy.

On July 14, 1928, Teller was planning to meet some friends at a Munich railroad station. He'd taken a streetcar from near the college and was lost in thought when he suddenly realized it was pulling out of the station where his friends were waiting.

In a hurry, he moved to the exit and leaped from the streetcar before it got up to speed. But the weight of his backpack shifted as he leaped, and he landed badly. As he fell to the ground, he breathed a sigh of relief that he'd managed to escape the trolley car's heavy wheels.

Or so he thought. In a 1978 interview, Teller described the moments after he made his jump.

"I saw the streetcar going by. I remember a sense of relief. And for a reason—I did not know, and I do not know—I did not try to get up but looked back. And then I saw my boot lying there, and I wondered, 'How will I go hiking?' And only after that, I looked at my foot that was gone and I wondered why I don't feel anything.

"And then I started to feel it."

Despite what could have been a devastating injury, Edward Teller refused to let the loss of his foot slow him down.

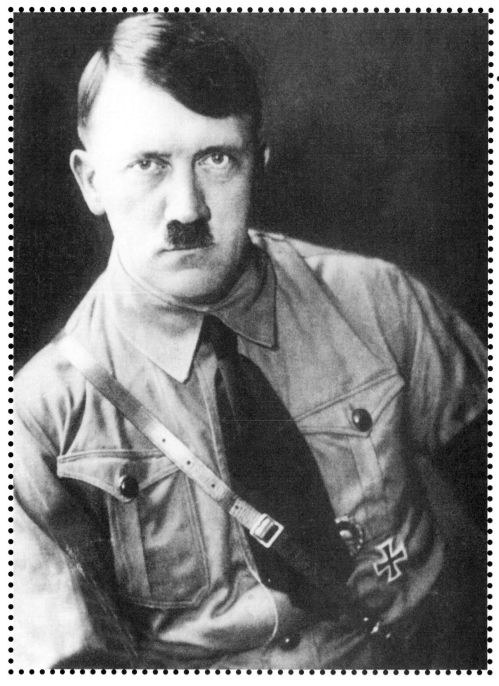

Adolf Hitler and Nazi anti-Semitism (or hatred of Jews) led to a mass exodus of Jewish scientists from Nazi territory. This loss of "brain power" was one reason the United States was able to surpass Germany in the development of atomic weapons.

Chapter 4
A Dangerous Time

• •

When a poorly timed leap from a moving street car cost Edward Teller his foot, he could have let it change his life. He didn't.

While his mother begged him to drop out of school and come home to recuperate, Edward refused. Instead he moved on with his life. He was fitted with a prosthesis—an artificial foot—and started walking again fairly quickly. He even took up table tennis and became an excellent player.

Teller once again made an academic move. Drawn to the work of a young professor named Werner Heisenberg, Teller again transferred, this time to the University of Leipzig.

"I could see in the beginning that he suffered from it [losing his foot], not just bodily but also mentally," Heisenberg told Teller's biographers. "But I think he overcame it rather soon. I think in a year or so he was quite stabilized in his mind."

While Teller's life quickly went back to normal after his accident, Germany itself was undergoing a rapid change.

Adolf Hitler was a failed house painter and World War I soldier who tried to overthrow the German government in 1923. After serving nine months in jail, Hitler began gaining popularity and power.

Hitler and the Nazi party that he founded were even more anti-Semitic than the governments of Teller's Hungarian childhood. By the late 1920s, many Jewish people fled Germany, often leaving with few of their possessions. Most chose poverty in a foreign country over the type of life they feared they'd have in Nazi Germany.

One of Teller's former professors, Herman Mark, managed to escape with his fortune intact. He used his savings to buy platinum wire—platinum is more expensive than gold—and fashioned the wire into coat hangers. Then he painted the hangers black and hung his clothes on them. At German checkpoints, the hangers were left alone.

At school, Teller often found himself in heated debate with fellow students. Many were fiercely anti-Communist and saw the Nazi party as the perfect defense against a system they hated. Teller saw evil in both extremes. To his way of thinking, democracy—the system of government practiced in the United States—was preferable.

In his final semester at the University of Leipzig, Teller got to meet his hero, Albert Einstein, when he traveled to Berlin to hear a speech given by the great physicist. Afterward the two met briefly, but as Teller recalled, "I listened, I didn't understand a syllable."

At the young age of twenty-two, Teller received his doctorate in physics from the University of Leipzig.

Dr. Teller considered several job offers in different parts of Europe, but despite the current conditions in Germany he decided to stay there. While life was becoming increasingly difficult for Jewish people, Germany was still at the forefront in scientific research. He took a job as an assistant professor at the University of Gottingen.

Meanwhile the Nazi party was gaining power.

Hitler's organization found support among the German people by pledging a return of the national pride lost after World War I. They promised to improve the economy by lowering prices and increasing employment. Many of the speeches given by Hitler and other Nazis blamed the Jewish middle class, who they claimed controlled banking and commerce. Their anger was aimed solidly at educated Jews like the new Dr. Teller and his parents.

In 1932, the Nazis became the largest political party in the Reichstag, which was similar to the United States Congress. In 1933, President Paul von Hindenburg gave Adolf Hitler the authority to form a new government. A few weeks later, the Reichstag building was destroyed by a fire.

Although the responsible party was never discovered—there is a strong possibility that the Nazis themselves set the fire—Hitler quickly blamed the communists because many Germans were afraid of them. In response to the fire, Hitler was given "emergency powers" so that he could maintain order. Free speech and free press were eliminated and most who had opposed Hitler in his quest for power were quickly imprisoned and even killed. Hitler's "Final Solution" called for the eventual extermination of all non-Aryans—people such as Jews, Gypsies, Catholics.

Among the Jews, scientists were hated the most.

Nazi Nobel laureate Phillip von Leonard called Albert Einstein "the most important example of the dangerous influence of Jewish circles on the study of nature."

As Germany became increasingly dangerous for him, Teller decided to leave. "The hope of making an academic career in Germany for a Jew existed before Hitler came and vanished the day he arrived," he told his biographers. He went first to the University of London to teach physics, and then to the Copenhagen Institute for Theoretical Physics.

On February 26, 1934, Edward married Mici in a small ceremony attended by their family and a few friends.

At his new job in the Copenhagen Institute, Teller worked under the supervision of Niels Bohr. Twelve years before Teller began at the Institute, Bohr had won the Nobel prize for physics—his ability was part of the reason Teller would later describe his time in Copenhagen as one of the most important periods of his life.

Bohr's and Teller's work focused on the atom, which was first described by the Greek philosopher Democritus around 400 BC. He believed that it was a hard particle so small it couldn't be divided. The word atom is from the Greek word "atomos," which means "that which can not be split."

Following Democritus, very little research was done on atoms until the 1800s, when English chemist John Dalton formulated the atomic theory of matter. Dalton said all matter consists of small bits called atoms, which are so small that billions of them could fit on the tip of a pencil.

But not all atoms are identical. There are 92 different kinds of atoms that occur in nature, and each kind is called an element. Examples of elements are hydrogen, gold and oxygen. Each element has only one kind of atom—gold contains only gold atoms and oxygen only oxygen atoms.

Many of these elements can be combined into what are called compounds. Atoms of two or more elements unite to form molecules. A molecule of water, for example, is composed of one atom of oxygen and two atoms of hydrogen.

Everything in the universe is made up of atoms, either as an element (such as lead) or a compound (such as table salt, whose molecules consist of sodium and chlorine atoms).

Most of Dalton's theories have stood the test of time. However, one of his theories would be successfully challenged. Dalton believed atoms could not be divided into smaller particles or changed. Disproving this theory would have a profound impact on the life of Edward Teller.

Atoms, it turns out, are not solid particles at all. They are mainly empty space and most of the atom's mass comes from its central core, called the nucleus. This is composed of two different particles—the proton and the neutron.

Whirling quickly around the nucleus, like a fast-moving planet in an orbit around the sun, are electrons.

In the late 1800s, Joseph John Thompson conducted experiments with a specially made glass cylinder called the Crookes tube. This glass tube is attached to a vacuum pump to eliminate the air. He experimented with the glow which occurred when electricity was shot from the negative metal plate on the one side to the positive plate on the other.

He learned that these "cathode rays are particles of negative energy. Atoms are not indivisible [they can be divided], for negatively electrified particles can be torn from their electrical forces. These particles are all the same mass and carry the same charge of negative electricity from whatever kind of atom they may be derived and are a constituent [part of] all atoms." Thompson was the first person to call those particles "electrons."

Thompson's student Ernest Rutherford discovered that the proton has a positive electric charge and electrons have a balancing negative charge. Rutherford's student would be Edward Teller's supervisor: Niels Bohr. Bohr would explain the motion of the electrons within the atom and way those orbits relate to the atom's energy level.

Only a few months before Teller's arrival at the Copenhagen Institute, James Chadwick, another student of Rutherford's, would prove the existence of the neutron.

All of the factors were in place when Teller chose atomic theory as the focus of his career. Although the time he spent at the Copenhagen Institute was very brief, the work he did there would have a enormous impact on the rest of his life.

In August of 1935, Edward and his new wife Mici boarded a ship and left Europe behind. He was headed for the United States, and eventually the heart of the atom.

A former Polish elementary school teacher, Marie Curie's discovery of radium would lead to a number of medical and scientific advances but would also cost her her life.

Chapter 5

Another World War

● ●

Years earlier, Max Teller had believed his son's fascination with math and physics would lead only to poverty and disappointment. He couldn't have been more wrong.

In 1935, Dr. Edward Teller was hired by Dr. George Gamow, whom he had met at the Copenhagen Institute, as a full professor in physics at George Washington University in Washington, DC. The job paid $6,000 a year, well over twice what most teachers earned. It came at the height of the Depression, a time in the US when the unemployment rate was more than 25% and work was scarce.

Teller began working in a new career, studying a science where discoveries occurred often: nuclear physics.

Completely unheard of just a few decades before, the study of atomic structure and the interaction of particles within the atom began with the work of a former elementary school teacher in Poland during the 1890s.

Marie Curie coined the word "radioactivity" to describe the radiation she discovered in a number of different elements. Prior to her work, it was believed that only uranium emitted radiation. Curie not only discovered this quality in a new element called radium, but also the work she did would lead to a variety of medical and scientific advances. Sadly, this radiation cost her her life in 1934.

Her work would inspire Lise Meitner, another woman who'd been encouraged by her Austrian family to pursue higher education. Years later, discussing how unusual this was, Meitner would say, "One realizes with some astonishment how many problems then existed in the lives of ordinary young girls, which now seem almost unimaginable. Among the most difficult of these problems was the possibility of ordinary intellectual training."

Despite the challenges, she earned her Ph.D. degree from the University of Vienna in Austria and moved to Berlin in 1907. Not long afterward, she become a full professor of physics at the prestigious Kaiser-Wilhelm Institute.

Her later work with a pair of Ottos—chemist Otto Hahn and her nephew and fellow physicist Otto Frisch—would lead Albert Einstein to call her "the German Marie Curie."

Like Einstein and Teller, Meitner found her own life threatened by Hitler's policies because of her Jewish faith but remained in Berlin until 1938. Managing to escape to Sweden, Meitner worked with the Nobel Institute of Theoretical Physics.

Otto Hahn, her partner in discovering a new chemical element called protactinium, stayed in Germany. In late 1938, Hahn and his assistant Fritz Strassman made a startling discovery during experimentation with neutrons.

Neutrons, because they don't have an electrical charge, can be "shot" into the nucleus of an atom like a bullet. In Richard Rhodes' book, *The Making of the Atom Bomb*, physicist I. I. Rabi explained, "When a neutron enters a nucleus, the effects are as catastrophic as if the moon struck the earth. The nucleus is violently shaken up by the blow, especially if the collision results in the capture of the neutron. A large increase in energy occurs and must be dissipated and this may happen in a variety of ways, all of them interesting."

After bombarding a uranium nucleus with neutrons, Hahn and Strassman thought they'd "chipped away" part of the uranium and somehow produced barium. However, that substance is only about half the mass of uranium, which made such an occurrence seem highly unlikely.

"There was nothing in the knowledge of nuclear physics to suggest that barium could possibly be produced as a result of the irradiation of uranium with neutrons," Hahn later explained in a biography of Niels Bohr.

So he sent a letter to Meitner. "Perhaps you can suggest some fantastic explanation," he wrote.

She replied, "Your results are very startling."

If it had been any other scientist, she would have assumed he'd made a mistake. But Meitner knew Hahn. She'd worked with him. She realized that Hahn's experiment hadn't just chipped at the nucleus of the uranium. He'd split it in two! Atoms could be divided, even changed, causing an enormous energy release to occur.

It was Lise Meitner who would first call this splitting of the atom "nuclear fission." She would also carefully calculate the potential energy release, relying in part on Einstein's theory of relativity. When she finished her calculations, she was astonished. She checked them again.

She'd proved it. A gram of uranium, under the right conditions, could release as much energy as many pounds of dynamite. Hahn's discovery could lead to a weapon of unimaginable consequence. And the Nazis were building it!

Otto Frisch repeated Hahn's experiment, checking for the energy release. He realized that during the bombardment the fission released two to three fresh neutrons, which could then bombard and split other uranium nuclei, each of which could release two or three more neutrons, and so on. Called a chain reaction, this process could lead to a new energy source—or a very powerful bomb.

Frisch shared the news with Teller's old boss, Niels Bohr, who told Teller. When he discovered that Werner Heisenberg, his mentor from the University of Leipzig, was leading the German nuclear weapons program, Teller was worried.

"I believe that urgent action [to maintain secrecy] is required," Teller was quoted in Rhodes' book. "Very many people have discovered already what is involved."

Teller went to Einstein with several other prominent scientists and convinced him to write the letter which would lead to the United States effort to develop this new weapon.

On August 2, 1939, in a letter to President Franklin Roosevelt, Albert Einstein explained the significance of the test. "This new phenomenon would also lead to the construction of bombs... A single bomb of this type, carried by boat and exploded in a port, might well destroy the whole port together with some of the surrounding territory."

Albert Einstein was right about the bomb's potential. He was wrong about how it would be delivered.

On September first of that year, any questions about the German government's intentions were answered. In a surprise invasion, the German army swept into Poland. Outnumbered and unprepared, the Poles were quickly defeated. Within a year, Germany controlled virtually all of continental Europe west of the Union of Soviet Socialist Republics, or USSR, the former Russia.

Roosevelt responded to Einstein's letter not long afterward and set in motion a series of events that eventually led to the development of the atomic bomb.

In the beginning, Teller wasn't so sure he wanted to work with the government. "To deflect my attention from physics, my full time job, which I liked, to work on weapons was not an easy matter," he told his biographers. "And for quite a time I did not make up my mind."

His attitude changed when President Roosevelt gave a speech on May 10, 1940 where he called on scientists to defend "our science, our culture, our American freedom and our civilization." Inspired, Teller began working as a consultant with the National Defense Research Committee.

Although the United States was still not officially involved in the war, government officials recognized the threat created by Nazi Germany. When this country entered the war following a surprise attack on Pearl Harbor by Germany's ally Japan on December 7, 1941, the effort to design an atomic bomb was already underway.

Code-named "the Manhattan Project," the effort would cost over two billion dollars in less than four years. This was an enormous amount of money sixty years ago, more than the value of the entire automotive industry.

The Manhattan Project consisted of several separate laboratories working toward a common goal.

In Oak Ridge, Tennessee, the newly discovered uranium isotope U-235 was separated from less fissionable (and thus less explosive) U-238. This was done by using a specially designed machine called a calutron, which relied on an electromagnetic field to accelerate the uranium atoms in a circle and separate the isotopes.

Meanwhile, Teller joined the University of Chicago effort to construct a nuclear reactor. This would help the scientists learn both how to control fission and how to sustain it. They hoped to achieve "critical mass," in which a precise amount of U-235 produces enough fresh neutrons to create a chain reaction when bombarded with neutrons. It was Otto Frisch, Meitner's nephew, who led this effort.

The reactor itself was built beneath the stands of the school's football stadium. After it became operational on December 2, 1942, the scientists discovered plutonium, a highly fissionable material which would soon be produced by nuclear reactors in Hanford, Washington.

Of all the laboratories working toward the atomic bomb, probably the best known was the one in Los Alamos, New Mexico. The lab was desolate and when Edward Teller arrived there it offered him the opportunity to be instrumental in making important scientific discoveries.

Unfortunately, the qualities which had once served him so well when he was a scientist working out his own theories alone in a laboratory created problems in the scientific community of Los Alamos. Teller kept his own hours, often working throughout the night, and sometimes kept fellow scientists awake with his 3:00 a.m. piano playing. He had a tough time fitting in.

Even worse, he wasn't interested in the bombs being built at Los Alamos.

These were atomic bombs, which used the principle of nuclear fission to achieve their explosive power. By the time Teller arrived at Los Alamos, he realized atomic bomb construction was inevitable. Already he had a new, much more powerful bomb in mind.

A few years prior, during lunch at Columbia University in New York City, Enrico Fermi and Teller discussed the work of Teller's boss, George Gamow. He'd been examining how stars generate their energy. Gamow discovered that light elements such as hydrogen in the stars fuse and create enormous energy when subjected to high temperatures.

Fermi wondered if this principle could be brought down to earth. Could an atomic bomb be used to create an even more powerful weapon, by exploding and causing the fusion of hydrogen to enormously increase the explosion's force?

In their conversation, Fermi mentioned a heavy hydrogen isotope called deuterium, which fused easily and was readily available in seawater.

Teller dismissed the idea. But as his research progressed and he became more involved in the effort to build a bomb, he began to reconsider his earlier opinion.

"Many of us had started to work on fission bombs," Teller told his biographers. "It had become clear that these atomic bombs would be powerful but expensive. If deuterium could be ignited, it would give a much less expensive fuel."

Teller went on to explain that "When Los Alamos was established as a separate entity, one of the arguments was that we would work on the fusion bomb as well as on the fission bomb. We actually didn't and this was certainly something that I was unhappy about."

Teller didn't hide his unhappiness. He would do important work at Los Alamos. He would calculate the amount of nuclear material needed for fission and prove that the efforts in Tennessee to separate uranium isotopes wouldn't accidentally trigger a nuclear explosion.

He also proved that the atomic bomb would not lead to a world-destroying chain reaction, providing a source of great relief for the scientists working on the project. But Teller really preferred working on the hydrogen bomb.

Because of the fears that Germany might soon have their own atomic weapon, every available scientist was put on the fission bomb.

In a 1954 interview with *Life* magazine, Teller's boss at Los Alamos, Hans Bethe, recalled that, "I hoped to rely very heavily on him to help our work in theoretical physics.

It turned out he did not want to cooperate. He did not want to work on the agreed line of research. He always suggested new things, new deviations. So that in the end there was no choice but to relieve him of any work in the general line of development of Los Alamos and to permit him to pursue his own ideas entirely unrelated to the World War II work."

Germany surrendered on May 8, 1945 without ever coming close to building an atomic bomb. Japan was still a threat, and the war, along with the Manhattan Project, continued.

On July 16, 1945, Edward Teller slathered on some sunscreen and placed welders' glasses over his eyes. He was 200 miles south of Los Alamos and a safe distance from test site Trinity, when Teller watched the first successful test of an atomic bomb. It was an awesome sight. A mushroom-shaped cloud blasted 40,000 feet over the desert sky as blinding light flashed below and the ground violently shook.

The bomb was a success. That single blast was equivalent to more than 20,000 tons of dynamite.

Dr. Teller and many others believed that if the Japanese could see what they had just witnessed, the war would effectively be over. A number of them lobbied government officials to demonstrate the weapon's power over an isolated area of Japan. Surely once Japanese officials realized how powerful the weapon was, they'd give up.

Dr. Robert Oppenheimer, the head of the work at Los Alamos and a Teller rival, disagreed. So did new President Harry Truman. A mere demonstration was considered too risky. If the Japanese still refused to surrender, a ground invasion would be the only alternative. Those responsible for planning the invasion knew that hundreds of thousands of American soldiers would die if that happened.

So an atomic weapon was loaded into the bomb bay of the Enola Gay, the B-29 aircraft that had been chosen to deliver it. On August 6, 1945, the plane flew over Japan and dropped the atomic bomb on the city of Hiroshima.

Luis Alvarez was a physicist riding in an airplane following the Enola Gay. His job was to use a device he'd invented in order to judge the force of the blast.

"I looked in vain for the city that had been our target," he wrote in a letter to his son Walter. "The cloud seemed to be rising out of a wooded area devoid of population."

Alvarez was sure there'd been an error and the bomb had missed. It hadn't. The destructive power of that bomb, and the one which followed it at Nagasaki three days later, vaporized buildings and killed over 150,000 people in a single blast of heat and light. Just as many would die later from illnesses caused by radiation.

The bomb worked. Japan formally surrendered on September 2, 1945. The work at Los Alamos to develop a nuclear weapon was over. Except for Edward Teller. Teller's work had just begun.

This photo of the atomic bomb shows smoke billowing 20,000 feet above Hiroshima on August 6, 1945. With a destructive force 1,000 times more powerful than the atom bombs dropped on Japan, Teller's H-bomb once erased an entire island from the face of the earth.

Chapter 6
Teller's Dream

● ●

When World War II ended, the United States was a country ready to celebrate peace. Soldiers returned home to their families, factories which had been manufacturing weapons of war began to produce consumer goods, and scientists began to leave Los Alamos.

Edward Teller wanted to stay.

The father now of two young children—Paul was born in 1943 and Wendy followed three years later—Teller had every reason to return to a quiet civilian family life. Except he had to find out if his theories about the hydrogen bomb would work.

According to his biography, Teller told the new director of Los Alamos, Norris Bradbury, that "I would remain only if the laboratory's intensive level of theoretical work could be maintained and channeled toward either of the goals—development of a hydrogen bomb or refinement of atomic explosions."

Bradbury couldn't make any promises. Even worse, Robert Oppenheimer refused to back Teller's goal. Disappointed, Edward Teller accepted a position at the University of Chicago, where he taught and published a number of important papers. Perhaps it was scientific instinct, perhaps it went all the way back to his childhood fear of communists, but Teller was certain the Soviets would soon have their own nuclear weapon.

Even though the US and the USSR had been allies during World War II, both sides distrusted each other a great deal and only their mutual objective of defeating Germany and Japan kept them together during the war.

On August 29, 1949 air samples collected off Japan's coast showed high levels of radioactivity. It could only mean one thing: Teller was right.

President Harry S. Truman issued a statement less than a month later: "We have evidence that in recent weeks an atomic explosion occurred in the USSR."

Teller was convinced that his bomb—which he believed would have a power 1,000 times of the atomic bombs dropped on Japan—would offer the United States protection from this new Russian threat. The US had reason to worry. In the years following World War II, communist governments allied with the USSR had taken over several countries in Europe. In 1948, the Soviets had tried to cut off access to West Berlin. Teller believed they would prove as dangerous as the Japanese.

Oppenheimer continued to oppose Teller's dream, saying in a letter to Harvard President James Conant, "I am not sure the miserable thing will work, nor that it can be gotten to a target except by ox cart."

Teller refused to give up. He told people that if he'd been allowed to work on the bomb uninterrupted it would have been finished by 1947. His passion didn't convince the government to move forward. Neither did it convince many of his fellow scientists and other citizens.

"My opinion at the time was that one should try to outlaw the thing before it was born," recalled Harley Rowe during later congressional hearings on the bomb. Rowe, a member of a committee on atomic weapons, said about the hydrogen bomb, "You are using it against civilization and not just against the military. I don't like to see women and children killed wholesale because the male elements of the human race are so stupid that they can't get out of war and keep out of war."

Besides its potential for destruction, many saw it leading to a future arms race, in which the USSR and the US would compete to build the best nuclear weapons.

In the end it wasn't Teller's passion, but Klaus Fuchs' deceit which convinced President Truman to go forward with the bomb. Fuchs, a German-born scientist who had worked at the Manhattan Project, was also a spy who had been supplying atomic secrets to the Soviets for several years. Because of his actions, the Soviet Union might already be close to their own "super bomb."

On January 31, 1950, four days after Fuchs confessed to his treachery, President Harry Truman sent a statement to the media which said, "I have directed the Atomic Energy Commission to continue its work on all forms of atomic weapons, including the so called hydrogen or superbomb."

Edward Teller returned to Los Alamos. There was a great deal of work ahead of him.

President Truman "gave the impression that we could produce a hydrogen bomb simply by tightening a few screws," Teller later complained. "Actually work had not begun. We had eight years of thermo-nuclear fantasies, theories, and calculations behind us, but we had established no connection between theory and reality. We needed a thermonuclear test."

Teller would have to bridge the chasm between calculations and reality.

The atomic bomb which had been tested at Trinity detonated at room temperature. The hydrogen bomb was called a thermonuclear weapon, because it needed temperatures in the tens of millions of degrees in order to ignite.

Thermonuclear reactions in the sun require temperatures of nearly twenty million degrees Celsius. The H-bomb would require even more heat, because the reaction would have to be faster. Unfortunately, the deuterium—the heavy hydrogen isotope found in seawater—would need an ignition temperature of over 400 million degrees Celsius.

The atomic bombs dropped on Japan had generated a temperature barely fifteen percent of what was needed.

Tritium, another hydrogen isotope, would fuse at a lower temperature. It was a very rare substance but if it was combined with the deuterium the bomb might work. Unfortunately, tritium was enormously expensive, basically defeating one of Teller's initial motivations for developing the bomb.

On June 25, 1950, Communist North Korea invaded South Korea. Fearing Soviet involvement, the United States government wondered if atomic weapons might again be needed. Spending excess money developing the hydrogen bomb looked like a bad idea.

Public opinion was also turning against the weapon, as "Ban the Bomb" signs began appearing everywhere. Einstein himself wrote that Teller's hydrogen bomb could lead to "radioactive poisoning of the atmosphere and hence annihilation of any life on earth."

Teller claimed his passion wasn't about a new weapon so much as the thrill of discovery. "One of my main reasons for working on the hydrogen bomb was its novelty," Teller said in his biography. "Not knowing how it would influence the future, I wanted both as a scientist and also for practical reasons to know how it would work."

On May 8, 1951, he got his first chance with an experiment known as the "George Test." The bomb at this point was very large, and would not work as a weapon. Still, it would be a test of the accuracy of the enormous calculations done by the scientists—calculations performed on a computer which took up an entire room, used 19,000 vacuum tubes and performed fewer functions than a modern calculator. It would also demonstrate to worried politicians in Washington, DC that the scientists who were using so much taxpayer money were making some progress.

The test was conducted on a desolate stretch of the Marshall Island chain in the central Pacific Ocean. Teller and his team waited through a three-hour rainstorm, then suffered another forty-five minute delay caused by an electrical short. The signal was given. The bomb exploded in a blast which vaporized both the tower and its concrete and iron supports.

A safe distance away, Teller watched quietly as the rest of his team whooped and hollered.

If Edward Teller believed the successful initial test of "George" would end the controversy, he was wrong. When the Chairman of the Atomic Energy Commission called a meeting at Princeton University in June, Teller wasn't invited to speak. For two days he listened as others described the work he'd done. "Finally I could contain myself no longer," Teller recalled in his biography. "I insisted on being heard."

Although several of the assembled scientists argued about it, Teller was finally able to speak. Two years later, in a congressional hearing, Gordon Dean vividly recalled the presentation Teller gave: "Out of the meeting came something which Edward Teller brought into the meeting with his own head. Which was an entirely new way of approaching a thermonuclear weapon."

Although his presentation impressed the scientists on that summer day, it had little impact at Los Alamos. Marshall Holloway was put in charge of the next test. Not only was Teller angry that someone else had been given the responsibility, he fought with Holloway on when the bomb would be ready. Holloway doubted they'd be set in nine months; Teller knew he'd be ready in six.

On November 1, 1951, Teller resigned from Los Alamos. Returning to the University of Chicago, he continued to speak with military and government leaders. Finally, Ernest Lawrence, the inventor of the cyclotron—a machine used to accelerate atomic particles—invited Teller to visit him in California.

Forty miles southeast of Berkeley, Teller toured a former Navy base. Over dinner Lawrence proposed a partnership, with Teller focusing on developing the hydrogen bomb.

The next week, Teller heard from both government officials and military leaders who felt a Teller-Lawrence partnership was a good idea. In Washington, Teller met with Secretary of the Air Force Thomas Kinletter and Secretary of Defense Robert A. Lovett. The Air Force was interested in sponsoring the project.

In March of 1952, The Lawrence Livermore National Laboratory was created by the National Security Council and the Atomic Energy Commission. Teller moved to California; in July he was joined by his wife and children. By then over one hundred scientists were working on the project. Teller was to oversee the design of the weapon; the team at Los Alamos would test it.

The bomb he was working on was much different from the one tested the year before. A mathematician named Stanislaw Ulam had suggested using two fission bombs. The second one would be detonated by the first to achieve the high temperatures needed for a thermonuclear explosion. Teller expanded on that idea and designed a bomb that even Oppenheimer, his longtime rival, called "technically...sweet."

If it worked it would be by far the most powerful weapon ever tested.

And Teller wouldn't watch.

Instead of traveling to the Central Pacific, Teller sat in a basement in California and waited for the seismograph in front of him to indicate the explosion's shock wave.

Similar instruments were placed by the Los Alamos team forty miles away from the 65-ton weapon, which was situated on the islet of Elugelab, part of the Eniwetok coral atoll. On Halloween 1952, when the bomb exploded, the mile-wide islet was vaporized.

There was nothing left. Teller's bomb was a success.

He quickly sent a telegram to his former associates that reflected his feelings about his fatherhood of the bomb: "It's a boy."

Dr. Edward Teller is shown here in March 1988 with then-President Ronald Reagan who was addressing a conference marking the first five years of his Strategic Defense Initiative program in Washington, D.C.

Chapter 7
Reckoning

· ·

T he question of whether or not Teller's dream of a hydrogen bomb was a good one will never be satisfactorily answered. After the first successful test of a hydrogen bomb, which wiped an island from the face of this planet and had an explosive yield of 10.4 megatons—700 times greater than the bomb which was dropped on Hiroshima—Teller and the scientists at the Lawrence Livermore Laboratory continued to test even more powerful weapons. These included a 15 megaton bomb less than two years later. It was the first hydrogen bomb tested which was deliverable, which meant that it could actually be used against an enemy.

The bombs themselves got progressively smaller, from the giant 65 ton bomb tested in 1952 to a small warhead which could be launched from a submarine. By the 1960s, bombs only a few feet long and weighing a few hundred pounds were developed. Lawrence Livermore lab itself would grow, reaching over 4,000 employees by 1961.

Teller would work on a variety of thermonuclear-related projects, including "clean bombs" designed to have little or no radiation. This idea never succeeded. Neither did atomic powered airplanes, nor the concept of utilizing hydrogen bombs for everything from redesigning landscapes to literally moving mountains. He also worked on promoting fusion as a possible energy source, a method still being researched.

In 1960, Teller accepted a job as a physics professor at the University of California. During his time there he developed what could become his most controversial idea ever. With evidence suggesting that the Soviet Union successfully tested their own hydrogen bomb—possibly in 1953, even before the United States—Teller came to believe that the best defense against nuclear weapons was to destroy them before they hit their targets.

Beginning with President Richard Nixon's Safeguard program in the late 1960s and continuing through the Strategic Defense Initiative, implemented in the 1980s by longtime Teller friend President Ronald Reagan, billions of dollars have been spent in developing an effective means of destroying nuclear weapons before they hit their targets.

But despite the enormous investment, no current anti-missile system exists and most such devices are banned by the 1972 Anti-Ballistic Missile Treaty.

Today, SDI is still front page news and Teller feels as he did in a 1969 interview with *US News and World Report* when he said, "I cannot tell you how much more I would rather shoot at enemy missiles than to suffer attack and then have to shoot at people in return. I want to repeat—with all possible emphasis—that defense is better than retaliation."

Now in his nineties, Teller is still Director Emeritus of the Lawrence Livermore Labs and a Senior Research Fellow at Stanford University's Hoover Institution.

On July 20, 1999, Edward Teller contributed to the millennium time capsule which was buried at Livermore, California. In a letter to the citizens of the year 2100 who will open it, Teller wrote, "The United States has won the Cold War without any bloodshed. This victory was made possible by scientific advances and technical progress that sufficed to eliminate violent confrontation between the US and the Soviet Union. This technical progress was due, to a considerable extent, to accomplishments at the Lawrence Livermore National Laboratory. The extent of the success is best understood by comparing the first and second halves of the 20th century. In the first half, the wars have killed people to the tune of at least 50 million. In the second half, loss of lives was reduced to a few percent of the 50 million.

"The explanation of the difference lies in the fact of weapons in possession of those who did not want to use them...I have confidence in the coming generations to believe that they will on the whole find a way to avoid misuse."

The generations who grew up in the twentieth century developed weapons capable of killing literally billions of people. It will be the responsibility of the generations who grow up in the twenty-first century to ensure these weapons are never used.

Edward Teller Chronology

- 1908, born to Max and Ilona Teller in Budapest, Hungary.
- 1914, enrolls in Mellinger School.
- 1918, enrolls in the Minta School.
- 1925, enrolls at University of Budapest.
- 1926, enrolls at Karlsruhe Institute of Technology.
- 1928, enters University of Munich.
- 1928, loses foot in trolley accident.
- 1929, transfers to the University of Leipzig.
- 1930, receives Ph.D. in physics from the University of Leipzig.
- 1930, hired as research consultant at University of Gottingen.
- 1932, takes assistantship in physics at University of London.
- 1934, marries Augusta "Mici" Harkanyi.
- 1934, joins Institute for Theoretical Physics in Denmark for eight months.
- 1934, returns to University of London.
- 1935, emigrates to United States and becomes physics professor at George Washington University.
- 1941, becomes an American citizen.
- 1942, joins Manhattan Project, first at University of Chicago, then at Los Alamos, New Mexico.
- 1945, witnesses test of atomic bomb.
- 1946, returns to University of Chicago.
- 1949, returns to Los Alamos for hydrogen bomb research.
- 1952, first H-Bomb successfully detonated.
- 1952, hired as consultant at Lawrence Livermore Laboratory.
- 1954, becomes Associate Director at Lawrence Livermore Laboratory.
- 1958, becomes Director at Lawrence Livermore Laboratory.
- 1960, becomes Professor of Physics at University of California.
- 1960s, first proposes missile defense system.
- 1975, retires from University of California.
- 1975, becomes senior Research fellow at Hoover Institute for Study of War, Revolution and Peace at Stanford University in Palo Alto.
- 1970s, promotes development of nuclear fusion as energy source.
- 1980s, promotes Strategic Defense Initiative, popularly known as "Star Wars."
- 1999, contributes to the millenium time capsule.

Hydrogen Bomb Timeline

- **400 BC:** Greek philosopher Democritus names the tiniest particles of matter "atomos," that which cannot be split.
- **1808:** English chemist John Dalton publishes theories on atoms.
- **1860s:** Dmitri Mendeleyev develops periodic table of the elements.
- **1895:** Conrad Roentgen discovers X-rays.
- **1896:** Henri Becquerel discovers uranium's radioactivity.
- **1897:** Joseph John Thompson discovers electrons.
- **1898:** Marie and Pierre Curie discover radium.
- **1900:** Max Planck develops quantum theory.
- **1905:** Albert Einstein publishes theory of relativity.
- **1908:** Hans Geiger invents radiation counter.
- **1920:** Ernest Rutherford discovers proton.
- **1932:** James Chadwick proves existence of neutron.
- **1938:** Otto Hahn and Fritz Strassman split uranium atom.
- **1939:** Lise Meitner coins term "nuclear fission," calculates enormous energy release.
- **1941:** Enrico Fermi proposes H-bomb theory.
- **1942:** First chain reaction nuclear reactor tested in Chicago.
- **1945:** Nuclear fission bomb tested; used on two cities in Japan.
- **1950:** Stanislaw Ulam proposes mechanical shock theory.
- **1952:** Ulam-Teller principle tested; history's first H-bomb detonated on November 1, 1952.

For Further Reading

Books

Berger, Melvin. *Atoms, Molecules and Quarks.* New York: G.P. Putnam and Sons, 1986.

Henderson, Harry. *Nuclear Physics.* New York: Facts on File, Inc., 1998.

Web Sites

www.achievement.org/autodoc/page/tel0int-1
www.llnl.gov/ask-teller
www.llnl.gov/llnl/02about-llnl/history.html
www.hoover.stanford.edu/BIOS/teller.html
www.sciam.com/1999/1099issue/1099profile.html
www1.onelist.com/group/doewatch/message/616

Glossary

Atom: smallest unit which makes up a chemical element.

Chain Reaction: neutrons from one atomic fission hit by nuclei trigger more fissions releasing still more neutrons.

Electron: tiny, negatively charged particle which comprises part of an atom.

Element: basic substance which cannot be broken down into simpler substances.

Fission: breakdown of atom's structure by "splitting the atom" because atom is "split" into about two nuclei.

Fusion: combining two atoms to form one heavier atom.

Ion: atom with an electrical charge.

Isotope: any two or more atoms of chemical element with the same atomic number but different mass and different behavior (such as uranium 235 and 238).

Molecule: combinations of different atoms which form compounds such as water.

Nucleus: center of an atom.

Neutron: uncharged particle found in the nucleus of an atom.

Proton: positive particle found in the nucleus of an atom.

Radioactivity: the ability of an atom to spontaneously emit energy or particles that spontaneously break down.

Reactor: device that uses controlled nuclear fission to create power or radioactive substances.

Index